AF078396

Books are for Reading, Not Eating!

No pages were eaten in the making of this book.
Disclaimer: If it wasn't clear from the title: Don't eat this book or any others

Copyright 2021, Steve Davala
All rights reserved
ISBN: 978-1-7370984-1-6

Books are for Reading, Not Eating!

By Laurie and Steve Davala

Illustrated by Francesca Da Sacco

There once was a girl, Liz McKeeting,
Whose favorite pastime was reading.
No more than a child
And sometimes quite wild,
Liz thought books
might make some good eating.

Her mom saw Liz go for a chew
And shouted, "That simply won't do!
Books are, Liz McKeeting,
for reading, not eating!"
And Liz went to bed feeling blue.

Still pouting, Liz turned down her lights,
Then spotted a book about kites.
She picked up the book
And with no second look,
She gobbled it up in three bites.

When Liz tried to hop out of bed,
A breeze blew her outside instead.
She knew she should care,
Feeling lighter than air,
That she now had a kite for a head.

Liz made it back down through the thunder.
Her mother yelled over her blunder:

"Books are, Liz McKeeting,
for reading, not eating!"
But now, Liz could not help but wonder.

If a book about kites made her fly,
What other fun things could she try?
She ate books about zoos,
About ships on a cruise,
And best yet, about hot apple pie!

"Delicious!" Liz thought with a grin,
"I've oodles of apples within."
She thought it quite cool
'Til she saw her dog drool
Then open his mouth to dig in.

"What now?" Liz cried out with a yelp.
"I've tried things from dragons to kelp.
Books are, Mom McKeeting,
for reading, not eating,
So please, I could sure use your help."

Her mom found poor Liz where she hid
With tentacles just like a squid.
She looked up and down
And searched 'til she found
An album of her precious kid!

The photos went down with regret.
A lesson Liz would not forget:
A book is indeed,
Not to eat, but to read,
But what of that new TV set?

www.ingramcontent.com/pod-product-compliance
Ingram Content Group UK Ltd.
Pitfield, Milton Keynes, MK11 3LW, UK
UKHW061139180426
11947UKWH00002B/10